Gold Rush

Hands-on Projects About Mining the Riches of California

Jennifer Quasha

The Rosen Publishing Group's
PowerKids Press™

Some of the projects in this book were designed for a child to do together with an adult.

For Ted, who makes my life rich.

Published in 2001 by The Rosen Publishing Group, Inc.
29 East 21st Street, New York, NY 10010

First Edition

Book Design: Felicity Erwin

Layout: Michael de Guzman

Photo Credits: p. 4 © North Wind Picture Archives; pp. 6 – 21 by Pablo Maldonado.

Quasha, Jennifer.
    Gold Rush : hands-on projects about mining the riches of California / Jennifer Quasha.— 1st ed.
      p. cm. — (Great social studies projects)
    Includes index.
    Summary: Projects and activities which illustrate the history of the California Gold Rush and pioneer life in that state.
    ISBN 0-8239-5705-5 (alk paper)
    1. California—Gold discoveries—Study and teaching—Activity programs—Juvenile literature. 2. Frontier and pioneer life—California—Study and teaching—Activity programs—Juvenile literature. [1. California—Gold discoveries. 2. Frontier and pioneer life—California. 3. Handicraft.] I. Title.

F865 .Q245 2001
979.4—dc21   00-027752

Manufactured in the United States of America

Contents

The California Gold Rush

Between 1848 and 1852, more than 200,000 people went to California looking for gold. These people were called gold **seekers**, or gold diggers. People went to California from different parts of North America and from around the world. In 1852, 81 million dollars worth of gold was uncovered. Still, the efforts of many **miners** did not pay off. Between the hard travel to California, false hopes, and difficult living arrangements, some seekers lost the desire to keep digging and went home. However, many stayed to help build California into a state. The gold rush brought people to California from all over the world, so that California became home to people of many different **cultures**.

The discovery of gold helped the United States become one of the richest countries in the world.

A John Sutter Mask

On January 24, 1848, gold was found near a **sawmill** owned by a man named John Augustus Sutter. Sutter had come to California in 1839. He wanted to start a farming business in America. Sutter built a sawmill by a river. One day, James Marshall, one of Sutter's workers, discovered gold. After the news got out, over 200,000 people came to California to seek gold. Here's how to make a mask of John Sutter:

tools and materials

- one sheet of white poster board
- scissors
- pink, brown, white, and red construction paper
- clear tape
- black yarn
- white glue
- single-hole puncher

1 Cut the shape of a head from the white poster board. Leave two tabs on the sides. Trace the "head" onto pink paper and cut out. Cut eyes from white and brown paper. Cut mouth from red paper.

 2 Tape eyes and mouth to pink face. Tape pink face onto white poster board.

 3 Cut out shape of nose and two small circles in the eyes that you can see through.

 4 Glue on yarn as hair, mustache, and beard. Punch hole into each tab using hole puncher. Tie yarn onto tabs.

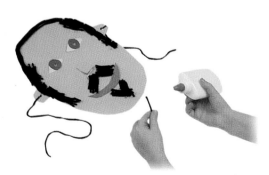

Gold Rush Poster

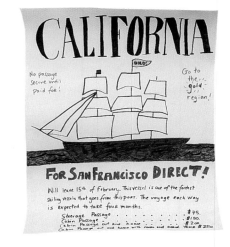

"Gold in California!" Those words sent thousands of people rushing to California from all over the world. People left their jobs and families to get even a little piece of the riches in California. Gold seekers traveled by land and sea. Passages through the countries of Panama, Nicaragua, and around the tip of Mexico were common. These trips were widely **advertised**. Here's how to make your own poster advertising the riches of California:

tools and materials

- two sheets of white poster board
- pencil
- masking tape
- magic markers
- ruler

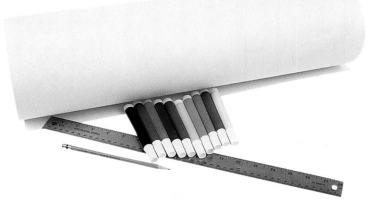

1 Using the pencil, sketch an advertisement onto the white poster board. You may want to tell people about your fast boats and wonderful prices. You may also want to remind them of the great treasure they will find in California.

2 Using the markers, color in your Gold Rush poster.

A World Map of Gold Seekers

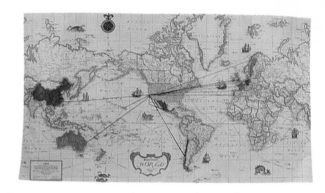

News of California's gold kept spreading. People rushed to San Francisco from other parts of the United States and from Europe, China, and Australia. All the gold seekers were forced to live together while looking for gold. Sometimes fights broke out because of different beliefs, **traditions**, and **religions**. Here's how to make your own world map of gold seekers:

tools and materials

- two sheets of white poster board
- masking tape
- world map
- markers
- ruler

Using the masking tape, tape two pieces of poster board side by side.

Mount the map onto the poster board by folding the edges of the map and taping them to the back of the poster board.

Find all the countries in the world where people traveled from to seek gold in California, then color in those places using the markers.

 Using the ruler, connect the countries to the port of San Francisco.

A Gold Rush Pan and Pieces of Gold

One of the easiest ways to find gold was by using a pan. Some pans were made out of wood. Later pans were made out of iron or tin. Miners would stand by the side of a river. They would scoop dirt and water into the pan and swirl it around. The water and small pieces of dirt fell through the holes in the pan, but the gold pieces would settle, or stay, in the pan. Here's how to make your own pan and gold pieces:

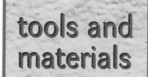
tools and materials

- aluminum pie dish
- pencil
- two paintbrushes
- gold and black enamel paint
- rocks and pebbles

1 Use the pencil to poke holes through the pie dish.

2 Paint pie dish black. Let dry.

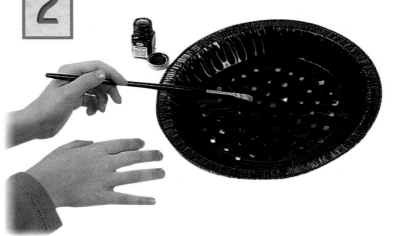

3 Using gold paint, paint the stones and pebbles. Let dry.

"Rough and Ready," a Gold Rush Town

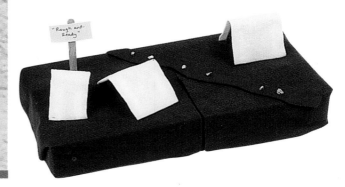

If one man found gold, it wasn't long before many others joined him. When a group of men found themselves living in the same camping area, they named their camps. Camps popped up everywhere with names like "**Poverty** Hill," "Last Chance," "You Bet," and "Rough and Ready." Many camps were set up by a river because the miners needed water for mining and to **survive**. Here's how to make your own Gold Rush town:

tools and materials

- one piece of white felt
- one piece of blue felt
- scissors
- seven Popsicle sticks
- white glue
- two pieces of green felt
- the top of a shoe box
- white paper
- black marker
- paintbrush
- gold paint
- pebbles

Using scissors, cut out three 2" x 4" (5 x 10 cm) pieces of white felt for tents. Then cut out a river from the blue felt. Break six Popsicle sticks in half.

 Using glue, cover shoe box top with green felt. Glue on the river. Glue the broken Popsicle sticks to tent felt as shown. Let the glue dry.

 Write "Rough and Ready," the name of the Gold Rush town, on the white paper, and glue to the unbroken Popsicle stick. Poke a hole in the top of the shoe box and place into hole. Stand the Popsicle-stick tents up on top of shoe box.

 Paint pebbles gold. After they have dried, glue into the river.

Gold Rush Playing Cards

When they weren't digging for gold, the men needed something to do. In town they often would meet in drinking **saloons** to drink and talk. Card playing and gambling often took place in the saloons. Card playing was also common in the camp grounds because it was an easy way to pass time and have fun. A pack of cards was very light, and the men could easily bring them wherever they went.

Here's how to make your own Gold Rush playing cards:

tools and materials

- poster board
- scissors
- pencil
- markers

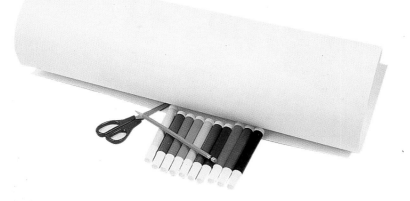

1 From the white poster board, cut five cards that measure 2 ½" x 4" (6 x 10 cm)

2 Using red and black markers, draw card numbers and symbols on the cards. For example, the three of hearts or the two of clubs.

3 Using the pencil, sketch Gold Rush scenes or objects on the back of the cards.

4 Using the markers, color in your drawings.

Gold Rush Scale

Gold had to be weighed to figure out its **value**. The gold was weighed on a scale. The person using the scale had measuring weights. These weights were in specific amounts, such as two **troy ounces** (62.2 g) or five troy ounces (155.5 g). The gold was placed on one side of the scale, the weights on the other. The person tried to balance the scale to find the gold's weight. Here's how to make your own gold scale:

<table>
<tr><td>tools and materials</td><td>

- X-Acto knife
- cardboard box
- balsa wood stick
- black paint
- paintbrush

</td><td>

- two bottle caps
- scissors
- thin wire
- gold paint
- pebbles

</td><td></td></tr>
</table>

Using X-Acto knife, carefully slice a hole in the top of the cardboard box. (Have an adult help you with this!) Cut a small slice into the top of the balsa stick.

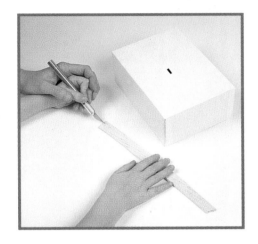

Using black paint, paint the cardboard box, bottle caps, and balsa stick. Paint half the pebbles with gold paint. These will be the gold. The unpainted ones will be the weights

Using scissors, cut four pieces of six-inch (15-cm) wire. Take two pieces and wrap around one of the bottle caps. Repeat with the other bottle cap.

Gold Rush Banking House

Once a gold seeker found gold, he wanted to change the gold into money. Sometimes gold was **acceptable currency**, but more often money was needed to buy things. Exchanging gold for money happened at a banking house. People had their gold weighed on scales, and then traded it for money. Whether they had found chunks of solid gold or hundreds of tiny flakes, gold seekers needed banking houses to turn their gold into money. Here's how to make your own banking house:

tools and materials

- one shoe box
- brown, white, red, black, and yellow felt
- one small cardboard (jewelry) box
- masking tape
- black, brown, white, yellow, red, and gold paint
- paintbrush
- 10 small pebbles
- four wooden clothespins
- googly eyes
- white glue
- two stamps
- small paper clock

20

Using white and brown felt, line the inside of the shoe box. Use white for the walls and ceiling and brown for the floor. Tape the top and bottom of the small jewelry box together and cover with brown felt.

 Using gold paint, paint pebbles. Using black, brown, yellow, red, and white paint, paint the clothespin people. Let paint dry.

 Using glue, glue on googly eyes and colorful felt arms.

 Glue in the clothespin people, gold nuggets, clock, and stamps.

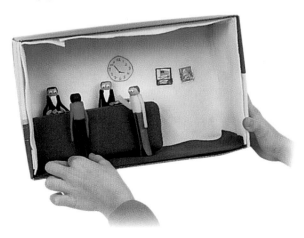

How to Use Your Projects

You have really struck it rich with these great social studies projects! You can hang your Gold Rush poster in your room for decoration. Maybe you and your friends can play with the Gold Rush playing cards on a rainy day. Are you studying about the California Gold Rush in your Social Studies class? Why not ask your teacher if you can put your Gold Rush scale or banking house on display in the classroom? It might help your classmates get a hands-on look at how gold was handled in the exciting days of the California Gold Rush!

Glossary

acceptable (ak-SEPT-uh-bul) To be gladly received.

advertised (AD-vur-tyzd) Announced publicly, often to try to sell something.

cultures (KUL-cherz) The beliefs, customs, art, and religions of a group of people.

currency (KUR-ent-see) The money in actual use in a country.

miners (MY-ners) People who dig into the earth to take out coal, ores, or other valuable things.

poverty (POV-er-tee) Being poor.

religions (REE-lih-jens) Beliefs in and ways of worshiping a god or gods.

saloons (suh-LOONZ) Places where alcoholic drinks are sold and drunk.

sawmill (SAW-mil) A building where trees are sawed into boards.

seekers (SEE-kurz) People who are looking for something.

survive (sur-VYV) To continue to live or exist.

traditions (truh-DIH-shuns) Ways of doing something that are passed down through the years.

troy ounces (TROYE ON-ses) A measure of weight used for gold. A troy ounce is heavier than a regular ounce.

value (VAL-yoo) The worth and importance of something.

Index

B
banking house, 20, 22

C
camps, 14

G
gold seekers, 5, 8, 10, 20

M
Marshall, James, 6
miners, 5, 12, 14

P
pan, 12

S
saloons, 16
scale, 18, 22

San Francisco, 10
Sutter, John Augustus, 6

W
weights, 18

Web Sites

To learn more about the California Gold Rush, check out this Web site:

http://ceres.ca.gov/ceres/calweb/geology/goldrush.html

24